Santiego Rivers

A LETTER TO MY FUTURE WIFE

A letter to my future wife

(I have been preparing for you)

Copyright © 2022 by Santiego Rivers

All rights reserved. This book may not be reproduced or transmitted in any form without the author's written permission.

"No copyright infringement is intended."

ISBN 979-8-9856180-3-7

ssrivers.com or Amazon

Dear Future Wife,

I never thought I would meet someone I could love, open and honest, who did not judge me or keep score of what I did wrong.

I never thought I would meet someone who would appreciate my effort to change over the time it took me to change, simply because they knew I was worth the wait.

The way you love me makes me want to love you even more because you have proven with actions what others could only deliver with words. **(Commitment)**

When it comes to you, I do not have to speak in parables or code, nor am I aloof with my feelings and emotions.

You bring out the best in me because you accept the parts of me that I am trying to change. My past is complicated, but my future is bright and clear with you in it.

This book will tell you about what I have learned on my journey to reach the only place I was destined to be, by your side.

A letter to my future wife.

They say a writer writes to express his feeling and emotions, so I will begin to pour out my pain which has transitioned to my love.

The main thing I want you to know about me is the following.

I never wanted to be who I am based upon the people that I was around at that moment, so I stayed to myself until I found the person, I could be myself with even at the risk of being alone.

I am the same person offline, that I am when I am online which is a rarity in this time, we currently live.

In this book, I am going to say things that may not make sense to other people but will make perfect sense to you.

This is the reason I consider you to be my better half!

Let me begin by telling you about my needs as a man.

I **need** the type of love that pain has caused to be pure. I **need** the type of love that rises like a phoenix from the burning ashes.

In so many words, I am trying to tell you why I **need** what you bring into my life. You compliment the parts of me that makes me give you all of me without you even asking.

You give me peace that makes the broken pieces of me whole. You touch the places deep down within me that only you can control.

You make me **need** to be a better man because you should never have to settle for less than a "Gentle" man.

You are everything I am not, but I am working hard to become.

I have always been hard on myself because somehow, I knew that something was within me better than me wanting to emerge.

I had to make peace with my pride and anger to realize that everybody has chapters in their life they do not want to read aloud.

It took me time to learn, but I eventually learned that the mistakes I made in my life gave me wisdom, and all the suffering I endured gave me the strength I needed to overcome the worse parts of me.

Me learning and growing from my past are why you now have the best part of me, and I am only getting better.

I was married once. I thought it would be forever, but even before I said, **"I Do,"** I already knew it would be tough.

In the beginning, I loved the way that she saw me, but unfortunately, the voices in her head and the whispers in her ears did not allow our marriage to survive the tough years that every relationship will face. Most people think problems within a relationship is a reason to throw or walk away from the vows you made to each other under the covenant of the Most High.

To me, it is like saying you will throw away a brand-new car because it ran out of gas or got a flat tire.

It does not make any sense to me!

When it came to my ex-wife, I admit parts of me wanted her back, but not the significant aspects of me that knew she did not deserve me back.

When a person shows you that they could easily walk out of your life, **you let them go**!

They say that pain makes you stronger, your tears make you braver, and the heartbreak you face makes you wiser.

After experiencing all these things and learning from them, I have become a better man.

I know that I am a better man because I know that it takes self-reflection, communication, understanding, and faith to make you realize that you will always be a work in progress.

I will forever be a work in progress because I choose to keep learning and growing!

I am not searching for perfection; I am not searching for physical beauty. I am just demanding **commitment** from my partner. I do not ask for anything I am unwilling to give, so I will never settle for less than the best a person must provide.

Meet me halfway, and I will carry you all the way back to the father!

Only my true soul mate was meant to understand these words because she knows the importance of each party fulfilling their roles in a partnership.

Your past is your past, but your future depends entirely on you!

I learned that if you do not leave your past in the past, it will destroy your future. So, I decided to live for today and not what yesterday has taken away.

It took my strength and courage to put the past behind me when she left me. I just had to remind myself that I deserved better because I knew I was worth it.

After my divorce, I did not try to get under someone else to forget about her. I did not want to forget about her. But, more importantly, I did not want to forget about the things I learned from being with her. I needed time to get my mind and heart back on the same page, so I took some time.

Sex complicates things when you try to clear up things in your mind. For example, I stopped being ruled by my little head long ago, which could be hazardous to a woman who thinks sex can control me.

I have learned that life will teach you lessons, even when you are not prepared to learn.

Even a fool could learn:

The valley of woe will teach you more valuable lessons than you will learn at the top of the mountain.

A wise man knows:

The top of one mountain is the bottom of the next mountain, so keep climbing!

What I learned from my past relationships was this.

Everyone I met before you were just everyone I knew before you. So, I had to be willing to learn from the mistakes I made in my past, so I would be ready, willing, and able to change and keep learning when I met you.

Success does not happen overnight. For example, *Thomas Edison* was not successful on his first, second, or even his hundredth attempt with the light bulb.

He just refused to give up because he knew it only took him being right one time to achieve success.

They say difficult roads lead to beautiful destinations. It must be true because I am standing here with you by my side, and I am satisfied!

In the beginning chapters of my life, I never knew that the pain, tears, and sorrow I faced would help me write new chapters in my story that became about us.

You were the light at the end of the tunnel that kept me moving forward, one step at a time.

In the journals of my life, what started as a horror story turned into a fairy tale once I learned to trust God's process to allow me the opportunity to remove the most significant obstacle out of my life.

(My fears)

I had to find the strength and courage to change myself for the better, or my fears would continue to change me for the worse.

I learned lessons on my journey because I lost a lot of time because of my anger and pride.

(I humbly say again)

I learned lessons on my journey because I lost a lot of time because of my anger and pride.

It takes a fool to lose what he loves for him to truly learn to love what he has left.

I know a lot about love because I have experienced so much pain in my life. I would not change a thing about the obstacles I had to overcome in my past because they all taught me lessons, I needed to learn to be worthy of having you in my life.

Having you in my life made going to hell and back worth it!

Let me tell you about the things I have learned.

I had to learn to stop asking for more things until I learned to master the fewer things I had in my life. Once you master what you already have in your life, God will bless you with more things to be grateful for.

I learned that God gives us the things we ask for, but not always in the ways we expect to receive them.

The following quote made me learn and appreciate gratitude.

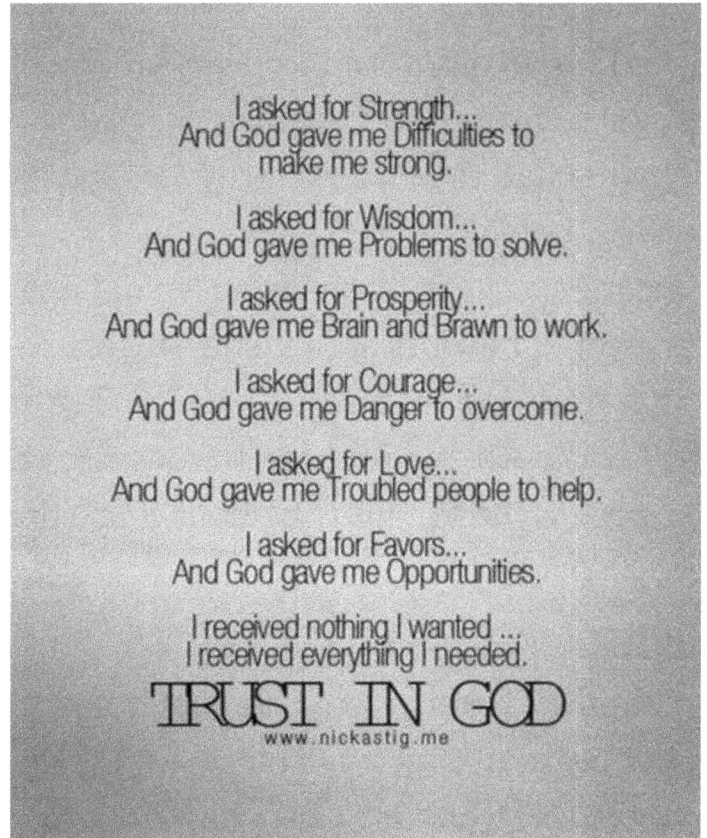

I asked for strength, and God gave me difficulties to make me strong. I have been hurt by people in my life who were supposed to love me unconditionally. I had to learn to forgive them because I would need to be forgiven at one point in my life. Facing this obstacle made me stronger than I ever was.

I asked for wisdom, and God gave me problems to learn to solve. The biggest problem I had to solve was why God gave me life. The pain I faced early in my life made me pray for death because I did not feel it could be worse than what my life was at that time. However, once I discovered why I was born and my life's purpose, it made me value the blessing of having a life here on earth.

I asked for prosperity, and God gave me the brain and brawn to work. First, I had to learn how to use my overthinking mind and my physical strength to help turn my dreams into reality. Just like faith without work is dead, thinking without acting will produce a bad outcome.

I asked for courage, and God gave me dangers to overcome. The most dangerous thing I ever had to face was me. Only I could be the villain in my life that would destroy it before it began, or I could be the hero who would save me from myself.

I asked for love, and God gave me people to help. By focusing on helping others, I realized that my life and my situation could be worse. I found both peace and happiness by helping others, which allowed me to help myself both mentally and physically.

I found my purpose in life, which was being in the service of others, which made me realize why I was created.

I asked for favors, and God gave me opportunities. Through all my trials and tribulations, I have come to understand that the only thing we should ever ask for is the chance and opportunity to become a better version of ourselves.

Once we learn to stop competing with other people and show gratitude, we will notice the chance and opportunity that God gives us each day we wake up.

The blessing is in the **wakening**! Finally, we get a chance to get it right!

In conclusion, to the things I wished for, I received nothing I wanted – I received everything I needed.

My prayers had been answered!

When we make a prayer to God, the only thing we need to do is prepare for the blessing.

Learning to say **"No"** is what shaped my future the most in my life!

I had to learn to say **"No"** to get the **"yes"** I wanted for my life.

My kind heart made it easy for those people with a taking nature to take advantage of me. I was desperate to be liked/ loved by others simply because I did not learn to like/love myself.

I had this problem for a long time in my life, so it took me a long time to address this issue.

I am still a work in progress when it comes to saying **"No"** to people I care about, but my self-esteem is much better now.

What I have learned in my process of personal development/ growth is this.

If you want to remove vampires from your life, learn to tell them **"No"** and watch how fast they will disappear into the darkness.

I have watched people scatter from my life like roaches do when the light turns on because I had developed the courage to say **'No"** to them and say **"yes"** to me!

Me saying **"No"** to the people in my life felt like I was spaying roach killer on them!

People will continue to keep using you until you stop letting them take advantage of you.

I am much happier today, even with me having fewer people in my inner circle. I now have you in my life, and it is enough for me.

Let me tell you about my "Why"

I always make my students explain their **"Why"** to me in their writing, so I would feel like a hypocrite if I did not explain to you why you in my life is enough for me.

Why having you in my life is enough for me

For this introvert, you do what a **"Type A** "personality person needs. You make things make sense in my life.

When this overthinking person tells you he is madly in love with you-you can assure that I have thought about a thousand reasons I should not be, but I still am.

I am in love with you!

You are the unexpected friend, lover, and companion I expected God to bring in my life if I was patient and faithful unto his words.

It was not always easy, but you were worth the sacrifices I made.

To be standing by your side, I have been to hell and back trying to find you.

I gave up hope a few times of ever having you in my life. I got tired of trying to fit my square peg in a round hole because, like **India Arie,** "*I was ready for love.*"

I wasted so much time, when time was the one thing, I knew I could never get back.

But still, I did not care because I was ready for love!

I was ready for the type of love that understood my wants and needs, but instead of fulfilling them, you helped me fulfill those things within myself.

You did this by reassuring me I was enough. I did not have to be anyone I was not. I only had to continue showing you who I was at my core and my willingness to change the things I needed to so my square peg would fit perfectly where it belonged.

We must be willing to remove our rough edges to become the people God created us to be!

I consider myself a good man, but I know I have my flaws

Most people are naive to think that a person can only fit into one category, even with knowing we are a dual nature creature.

Most people assume a good person is without flaws and a bad person is without morals and integrity.

The Christian in them forgets that *Lucifer* was the most beautiful angel in heaven before he was considered a horrible beast.

I am no *Lucifer*, but I am no *Michael* either. I am merely a man whose emotions tend to get the better of him more times than I would like.

The Most High is still working on me

There are some people who can and will point out all the things they feel I did wrong to them or in my life.

Those same people will never admit or speak about what I did to correct my negative actions or words in those situations. I have no problem apologizing.

I am not in denial of the fact that I have wronged people in my life and burned bridges I may never be able to repair.

I accept my faults and I apologize for acting out of character regardless of the reason. With that being said, **I refuse to allow anyone to hold me to my past!**

I have **morals** and a **conscious**. I do not make it a habit of hurting people or being rude or unkind.

By nature, I try to avoid conflict. I would be willing to say I am wrong or merely exit the scene instead of getting into a confrontation with anyone over anything where emotions are involved. I know my temperament and I know what I would do if I felt disrespected.

I learned you must be careful of arguing with a fool in public because the bystanders may find it hard to identify the foolish person.

When we allow our emotions to overrule our ability to think, no good can come of it.

There are people in prison or in their grave over losing their temper in the heat of the moment. They did not realize that what is did out of anger could cost you your life.

I try my best to be slow to anger because I know what dwells within me

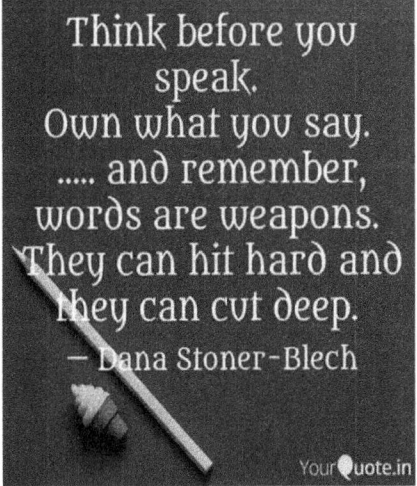

In my early years, I made the same mistakes more than a few times. The older I got, I realized the importance of thinking before I spoke or acted.

I do not like to apologize, but I would do it instantly if I did something to someone that caused them grief or pain.

To avoid the need of apologizing so often, I have become careful of my words or actions, including doing the same negative thing over and over.

I did mention earlier that The Most High is still working on me!

I have my good days and I also have those days where I pray heavily!

Life has taught me what only time could teach someone with a hard head. Life has taught me the difference between a mistake and a pattern which becomes our habits.

The only habit I want to be known for is treating other people the way I want to be treated in return.

I am a big believer in karma!

I have done so much in my past; I cannot afford to add to my tally or to the weight in my heart.

I must be careful of how it will measure in the end!

God knows my heart, but I know I am responsible for my actions.

Most people are self-serving

The people who will tell you negative things about me will never tell you what they did to bring out the worse in me or how I treated them before we stopped dealing with each other.

As I mentioned earlier, I know I am responsible for my actions, I just need you to know I do not act most times without a reason.

Especially when it comes to me acting in anger.

I have learned that anyone who is quick to tell you about the faults of others have faults of their own.

I have learned the hard way to be careful who you give to, whether it is your time, money, or attention because takers will keep on taking.

The people who have a problem with me is because I learned to say **'No"**!

I cannot change how people from my past feel about me or the people in the present who is not part of my *inner circle*.

I only care to make sure that when it comes to you, my words match my actions and I am doing everything in my power to make sure you feel loved, appreciated, and wanted, even when we are not agreeing completely.

In every relationship, there will be problems. I plan on being by your side, for better or for worse. The one thing I know I will probably **"NEVER"** be strong enough to deal with is you allowing someone else to come between us.

My father and I have a big problem with that. **(Exodus 34:14)**

Let us get some understanding

Trivial things will become massive things in a relationship.

The following things are important for couples to agree on before exchanging vows because these issues are not going to disappear or solve themselves.

Bills / Parenting style / credit & debt / Religion / How to deal with family / Childhood trauma / fears /sexual expectations / partner expectations /financial expectations / health history /mental health issues / Bucket list / political views / What to do if we cannot figure something out between us

Partner expectations

I am not looking for someone to complete me. I was waiting for someone to compliment the greatness already within me and understand I am a work in progress.

I used to think that another person was going to make me a whole person until I realize that if they left me, I would not be complete anymore.

Therefore, we must learn to love ourselves independently of anyone else loving us.

I love me some me! This is the type of mindset I developed over time. I learned to never put your happiness in the hands of someone else.

The only thing I want from a partner is someone I can trust with my dreams and fears, and respect me as her man.

I do not want to always have to be something I am not because you cannot except me for who I am.

I am not always strong, but I am not always weak. I may not always like what you do, but I will always love you. I do not expect anything from my partner that I am not willing to give in return.

Financial expectations

I think that being partners mean being partners in every aspect of your life. A good leader learns to utliize the people on their team.

If you are stronger at handling the finances and you want to be in control over the money and budgeting, I will follow your lead.

Being a leader does not mean that you are always in control of everything. I only expect that we work together and produce a plan that will help us achieve the goals/dreams we desire. **Communication** is especially important overall.

Bills

When it comes to paying bills in the home. I feel that both parties should do their part based upon the agreement we made. I understand that situations change which is why it should never be assumed that one person is responsible for everything.

Parenting style

I believe in giving our kids a hand- up, not a handout. Most of my kids are grown, so the only person I feel financially obligated to is my wife. I will not take away our house money to give it to our kids unless you agree on it. We are a united front, which means we parent together!

credit & debt

We should know where we stand when it comes to *credit and debt*, so we can produce a plan to fix it. Life happens, so we need to address it as a team.

Religion

I am not a religious person; I am a spiritual being. I do not push my belief on anyone because everyone is responsible for their own soul.

I currently do not attend any church nor am I opposed to going with you. I love learning and hearing different perspectives.

I am not an *Atheist* or *Mason*, but I do possess the knowledge of a *"Traveling Man,"* I know my **(B)**asic **(I)**nstructions **(B)**efore **(L)**eaving **(E)**arth, and I know that *Egipt* is in Africa.

I do not have to be preached to -to learn the things that are important to me. My spiritual well-fare is particularly important to me. If you have seen my library in my home, you would know, I am always studying to show myself approval. I did not create a **heaven** or **hell** to put anyone in, so I could never tell a person what to believe in. The important thing is to believe in something, in my opinion

How to deal with family

I am remarkably close with my family, and we spend a great deal of time together. Even with that being said, I do realize the importance of you and I having our own life and plans that only involve us.

My first and last priority is to you and the life we have together. I will not let family or friends come between us and our relationship.

I have seen firsthand what could happen when a family member does not like your spouse, how it affects the relationship.

The whisper in their ears becomes the voices in their head that tells them that the person they love is no longer good enough for them.

Childhood trauma

Most adults walk around with trauma. Trauma from our childhood that goes unresolved often follow us into our adulthood and our relationships.

When we do not address the issues, we are facing, those issues become baggage's that we carry around with us.

No one can fix issues that they did not cause, nor should they be responsible for dealing with the problems you are not willing to come to terms with yourself.

The person in your life should only be willing to support you on your journey to recovery. If you are not willing to help yourself, how can anyone else do the job you are not willing to do for yourself?

You are responsible for being your own hero. Your companion should only be your sidekick who stands by your side on your journey.

- **Seek help!**
- **Seek counseling!**

Surround yourself with people who support and push you, not people who drain you or add on to the burdens you already carry.

The people you need in your life are the ones who will stay on you to get the help you need.

The issues you keep running from will be the anchor that holds you back from reaching your destination.

It took me years to be willing to address my own personal issues, but when I finally did, it was worth it.

Everyone must get to a point in their life when they realize that the way they are currently doing things is not working for their benefit.

Until you are willing to change your life for you-you will always be the biggest problem in your life!

Fears

I learned that the fears we do not face becomes our limits. Having this understanding is why I started attacking the things that I feared.

What we hold onto we eventually become. I did not want to become the things I feared. I used to fear death, but now I only fear not living the life God created me to live.

This is the reason I am always trying to change myself for the better. I do not fear loving you with all my heart simply because I have been hurt in the past.

I was hurt by others in my past simply because it was supposed to happen. When we do not move or change the things that God needs us to change, he will do it for us.

Everyone serves a purpose in your life. The people who were meant to stay in your life, will fight to be in your life.

God will do the things for us we are not willing to do for ourselves. He heard the things we did not hear, including seeing the plans that would not serve us for the better.

We should not waste our time hating those people. They merely served their purpose in our life, and now it was time for us to move on.

Therefore, God removed those people from our life by allowing them to cause us pain. We learn more from our pain than we learn from anything else.

"We are crazy like that"

I learned to trust God without question because I know that he did not bring me this far to leave me standing alone.

I still have my struggles and doubts, which is why I say the *"Serenity Prayer,"* in those moments.

Sexual expectations

I do not believe sex should be used as a weapon to control our partner. This is one of the reasons why they say, do not go to bed mad.

We are physical beings which means that we crave or desire the physical touch of others.

I think the more you touch or hold your partner, the closer and the less problems you may have in the relationship.

When you are kissing or snuggling with your partner, how does it make you feel? You should feel at peace and loved.

A couple that fights often do not spend a lot of time snuggling or merely holding hands.

You need to work on being close instead of worrying about being intimate, sexually.

We all have our own expectations which should be talked about openly.

Take the time to get to know your partner and allow them to get to know you. Be open and understanding to what turns your partner on.

Communication does not stop when you reach the bedroom. You should learn to communicate / talk more in the bedroom, including laughing. **(Act a fool)**

Take away the pressure of having to always perform at your best. No one is always going to hit the ball out of the park every night, but I know that there are a few people who will.

I am not that person!

(Unless there is music playing. I will then perform)

Old habits die hard!

Physical & mental health issues

Never get into a intimate relationship with anyone who is not actively or willing to address their physical or mental health.

You will never be able to help anyone who is not willing to help themselves. It is not your job to save anyone, but yourself.

The same person you are trying to help will eventually look at you as their enemy, even though you are only trying to be supportive.

A person will only change or seek help when they are ready. I know that this may be hard for people with a big heart to accept. I also know that there are exceptions to every rule.

You do not want their problems to become your burden because when you both are struggling, who will save the both of you?

Help someone when they are willing to help themselves, by seeking counseling or a doctor.

Political views

People can coexist with someone who does not always agree with their point of view. You should make sure that you find someone who believes that it is okay to agree to disagree respectfully.

You will not always agree with everyone you meet. Sometimes you may even disagree with yourself. The mind and the heart seldom agree with each other.

Stop trying to find another you in someone else. Iron sharpens iron. Understand the meaning behind that and it will give you a better perspective about agreeing to disagree respectfully.

Bucket list

Your dreams are your dreams, and your partner dreams are their dreams. You do not always have to share the same dreams and goals.

What you should share are dreams and goals that requires the both of you working together to achieve them.

Life is meant to be lived. As you chase your dreams, allow your partner to chase their dreams, and the both of you can enjoy the journey together.

Create a vision board, which is the same as a written bucket list. Take turns achieving the goals and dreams off both of your vision board together.

If you spend more time chasing/ following your dreams, you have less time to fight and worry about what other people think or feel about your relationship.

Friends of the other sex

The only other man I want to be close to my wife is **Jesus**! Just like women knows women, men know men!

Do not put me in a situation where I feel disrespected by your single male friend.

I understand that there must be trust in a relationship, but the question I would ask my partner is, do that man have feelings for you?

I do not play having a work husband, gym husband or any other husband beside me. **I do not like to share**!

A real friend would know to fallback when you are in a relationship. Your friend better know to fall back when you are in a relationship with me if he is a straight and single male.

I am joking, but I am dead serious!

If you are going to have single male friends, we all need to sit down and talk about boundaries because I do not want anyone to be surprised when I act a fool!

I do not want to hear that he was just playing, or he did not mean anything by it.

Like I told you earlier, I am just like my father. **(Exodus 34:14)**

I have no problem going to counseling over this issue.

Yes, I will admit that I am telling you that I probably can't be friends with a single female if I am in a relationship because I don't want those problems in my life.

Do not make me go "Will Smith" on someone!

I understand if you have kids with someone or some other circumstance. I just need for us to have an understanding and we all sit down and talk.

It is important that both of you understand, *I say what I mean, and I mean what I say.*

Do not make yourself available for another man and I will not make myself available for another woman.

Please help keep me out of prison or the grave!

What to do if we cannot figure something out between us

What to do when you and your partner cannot agree or figure things out between the both of you? Take your problems to God.

God is the only other person in your relationship whose opinion matters. Pray on it separately, including together with your mate.

You both must ask yourself will you allow the problem you are currently facing be bigger than the relationship itself?

You both must be willing to put your ego (E.G.O) to the side because it is only edging God out of your relationship.

It is better to lose some battles if it allows you to win the war. Your marriage/relationship is the war you should always be fighting to win.

Therefore, couples should have or create a **"War Room"** in their house to take all their problems to.

The enemy wants to see your relationship fail, so you will turn to them instead of depending on each other.

I am not telling you what I think, I am telling you what I know from my own experience. Do whatever it takes to save your union despite the displeasure of other people.

The people whose opinion you should value will tell you the same thing.

The information in this book is not meant to solve all the problems that we will face overtime.

The information in this book should give us a foundation to build upon and refer to when we face the challenges life will present us.

I want this book to remind us of the importance of talking and listening to each other.

I want us to remember to listen to each other for **understanding** and not to be able to **reply** in defense.

Before we were lovers, we were best friends. If we remember to be friends, we will have a good chance of growing together instead of growing apart.

Our union will take work, sacrifice, and tears to make it to the golden years of a marriage.

I want us to seek couple counseling throughout our marriage and put the work into saving our marriage before real trouble arises.

I want to have friends who are married to talk about married stuff and get suggestions on ways we can better our union.

I understand that all our friends will not be married, and we will not share the same friends.

Sometimes it takes listening to other people to realize that the problems we are going through is minor to what other people are facing.

I want our marriage to work. With that being said, I am telling you that I am willing to put in the needed work.

I just need you to meet me halfway!

Santiego Rivers

A LETTER TO MY FUTURE WIFE

www.ingramcontent.com/pod-product-compliance
Lightning Source LLC
Chambersburg PA
CBHW060035180426
43196CB00045B/2688